SCOPES:

CREATION ON TRIAL

R.M. Cornelius
and
John D. Morris

Master
Books

First printing: May 1999

ISBN: 0-89051-257-4
Library of Congress Number: 99-70691

Interior photos courtesy of Bryan College, Dayton, Tennessee

Cover by Janell Robertson

Previously published by Institute for Creation Research.

Printed in the United States of America

Contents

1. Their Stage Drew All the World 5

2. Mr. Bryan on Evolution 25

3. The Dayton Deception 31

4. The Effect of the Evolution "Victory" 47

CHAPTER 1

THEIR STAGE DREW ALL THE WORLD

A New Look at the Scopes Evolution Trial[1]

by R.M. Cornelius

Defended by some and denounced by others, the Scopes trial of 1925 not only was a major event covered by some two hundred newsmen (whose stories totaled about two million words), but also became a reference point for a series of similar legal controversies in at least seven states. In addition, it served as a major influence on the de-emphasizing of evolution in high school biology textbooks up until 1960.[2] The significance of the trial was further recognized, first in 1977 when the trial courthouse was designated by the National Park Service as a National Historic Landmark, and then in 1979 when a one-million-dollar courthouse restoration and trial museum project was completed. Although the renovation of the 90-year-old courthouse was long overdue, no less overdue is the revelation of the real story behind the trial.

Since 1925, the Rhea County Courthouse has been famous as the stage for the "Monkey Trial" of John Thomas Scopes, accused of teaching evolution in Dayton, Tennessee, a small town nestled among the Cumberland Hills 40 miles north of Chattanooga.

---

1 Revised and reprinted with permission from *Tennessee Historical Quarterly*, 40, Summer 1981: 129–143.

2 Judith V. Grabiner and Peter D. Miller, "Effects of the Scopes Trial: Was It a Victory for Evolutionists?" *Science*, 185, September 6, 1974, 832–837.

Rhea County Courthouse — site
of the Scopes evolution trial.

Many actors and action lines played a part in this legal drama, described by the title of one book as *The World's Most Famous Court Trial.*[3] a three-time presidential candidate, America's foremost criminal lawyer, the 20th century's most cynical journalist, evolution versus religion, academic freedom, and government authority versus parental rights.

Seeking juicy morsels for their omnivorous readers, journalists at home and abroad have periodically descended upon Dayton like the wolf on the fold. But the pressures of deadlines or of editorial bias have tended to keep many of these analysts from getting to the heart of the trial. Consequently, this courtroom performance is known chiefly for its famous characters, fabricated conflicts, and fiery climax rather than for its intrigue-filled prologue, essential issues, and influential epilogue. In their willingness to serve the public a superficial sop, the sunshine reporters and summer researchers rarely discovered or acknowledged that for the citizens of Dayton, the real reason for the trial was not evolution, religion, or academic freedom; it was economics. As explained by Warren Allem in a University of Tennessee history thesis, the trial began as a public relations scheme to interest a second generation of developers in the industrial potential of the Dayton area.[4]

When George W. Rappleyea, a young metallurgical engineer with the ailing Cumberland Coal and Iron Company, picked up his May 4, 1925, copy of the Chattanooga *Times* and read an announcement of an American Civil Liberties Union offer to pay

3 William Hilleary and Oren Metzger, eds., *The World's Most Famous Court Trial: Tennessee Evolution Case* (Cincinnati, OH: National Book Co., 1925).

4 Warren Allem, *Backgrounds of the Scopes Trial at Dayton, Tennessee* (unpublished M.A. Thesis, University of Tennessee, Knoxville, 1959). Parts of this account were discussed in "Scopes Trial a Setup to Rescue Town," R.M. Cornelius, *Atlanta Journal and Constitution*, May 7, 1978, sec. A., p. 1, 22, and 26, and are reprinted with permission.

Left to right: John T. Scopes, Dr. John R. Neal (defense), and George W. Rappleyea (trial instigator).

the expenses of a teacher willing to make a test case of the recently passed Tennessee anti-evolution law, he knew that a powerful remedy for the limping local economy had been discovered. Rappleyea hurried over to discuss the article with F. E. Robinson, "The Hustling Druggist." Teacher John T. Scopes and superintendent of schools Walter White were brought in for consultation. The next day, May 5 — the day the case supposedly began as a result of a "chance" meeting at Robinson's Drug Store — lawyers and town officials were drawn into the plot. Scopes agreed to act as the law-breaking villain and was promptly served with a warrant.[5]

The casting of the principals was complete when three-time presidential aspirant William Jennings Bryan accepted the invitation to help with the prosecution and when criminal lawyer Clarence Darrow and New York divorce lawyer Dudley Field Malone volunteered their services to manage the defense. Bryan was invited partly because the Dayton promoters had an eye for the spectacular and partly because some people wanted to acknowledge Bryan's influence in getting the anti-evolution law passed. The former Secretary of State, Democratic Party leader for over 20 years, and popular Chautauqua orator, had lectured in Nashville on "Is the Bible True?" the year before the Tennessee legislature considered Representative J.W. Butler's bill to make it "unlawful for any teacher in any of the Universities, Normals,

Clarence S. Darrow.

---

5 Allem, *Backgrounds of the Scopes Trial*, p. 55–61.

Left to right: George Rappleyea, Walter White (Supt. of Schools),
F.E. Robinson, and Clay D. Green (teacher).

and all other public schools of the State which are supported in
whole or in part by the public school funds of the State, to teach
any theory that denies the story of the Divine Creation of man as
taught in the Bible, and to teach instead that man has descended
from a lower order of animals."[6]

Darrow was appealing to some of the Dayton impresarios
— if not to the ACLU — because of his reputation as a crafty,
successful defender of difficult cases. But, practically speaking,
perhaps the main reason for the confrontation between Bryan
and Darrow in Dayton was the role of the press, as spotlighted
by Warren Allem, newspaper columnist; radio commentator Jef-
frey St. John; and trial historian L. Sprague de Camp, who noted
that some reporters grew their own news stories by planting sug-
gestions in the minds of Bryan and Darrow about trial participa-
tion, by cultivating the ground for quick sprouting, and by har-
vesting them as fully ripened decisions even before they were
half developed.[7]

The prologue continued when others, in addition to George
Rappleyea and his collaborators, recognized the potential box
office appeal of the trial. On May 18 and 19, Chattanooga lead-

---

6   John T. Scopes and James Presley, *Center of the Storm: Memoirs of John T. Scopes*
    (New York: Holt, Rinehart, & Winston, 1967), p. 52.

7   Allem, *Backgrounds of the Scopes Trial*, p. 63.
    Jeffrey St. John, "The Significance of the News Coverage of the Scopes Trial," ad-
        dress given at the Dayton Chamber of Commerce annual meeting, March 20,
        1979.
    L. Sprague de Camp, *The Great Monkey Trial* (Garden City, NY: Doubleday, 1968),
        p. 80, 89–99.

ers tried first to get the trial moved to their Memorial Auditorium, and, when that plan failed, they attempted to set up a case involving a Chattanooga teacher. The Dayton entrepreneurs countered by calling Scopes home from vacation in Kentucky, arranging a special meeting of the grand jury instead of waiting until the regular session in August, and planning a protest meeting to maintain public interest.[8] They announced that one part of the meeting would be a speech by Rappleyea on behalf of evolution; but they did not reveal that Rappleyea was not an evolutionist[9] and had secretly arranged to be interrupted by a fight staged by a local barber, Thurlow Reed, whose shop was across the street from Robinson's Drug Store. When Rappleyea said, "There are more monkeys here in Dayton than there are in the Chattanooga zoo," Reed shouted, "You can't call my ancestors monkeys," and began a tussle with Rappleyea that apparently fooled everyone and earned Reed the title of the "man-biting barber."[10] After the intrigues of this backstage action, the prologue to the trial was over.

By the time Act 1 opened with the gathering of the participants and the audience, the trial, whose basic plot had been conceived in the New York offices of the ACLU and whose script had been written in a Dayton drug store, was becoming something of a *tour de farce*. In contrast to the conglomeration of notables who made up the ACLU executive planning committee — future Supreme Court Justice Felix Frankfurter, socialist Norman Thomas, Communist Party member Mrs. Elizabeth Gurley Flynn, Father John Augustine Ryan, Roger Nash Baldwin, and Arthur Garfield Hays — there were the following who circulated among the mixed multitude at the Dayton spectacle: Joe Mendi, the trained chimpanzee; Deck Carter, "Bible Champion of the World"; and Lewis Levi Johnson Marshall, "Absolute Ruler of the Entire World, Without Military, Naval, or Other Physical Force."[11]

Media representatives were there, too. Radio men from the

8 Allem, *Backgrounds of the Scopes Trial*, p. 65–66.
9 Telephone interview with Juanita Corvin Tennyson, Rappleyea's niece, May 25, 1977.
 Telephone interview with Giles Ryan, who attended all sessions of the trial, May 30, 1977.
 Personal interview with Ferrell Reed, son of Thurlow Reed, July 10, 1980.
10 Allem, *Backgrounds of the Scopes Trial*, p. 67–69.
 Personal interview with Ferrell Reed, July 10, 1980.
11 de Camp, *The Great Monkey Trial*, p. 163–164.

Joe Mendi, the chimp, plays for his handler and neighborhood girls at the Scopes trial.

Chicago Tribune's WGN arrived for what was to be the first national broadcast of an American trial. Sixty-five telegraph operators moved in and began sending more words to Europe and Australia than had ever been cabled about any other American happening. H.L. Mencken, Joseph Wood Krutch, Westbrook Pegler, and almost two hundred other reporters thronged the press box, some of them "unofficially acting in behalf of the defense,"[12] having received editorial directives as to how the trial was to be played up in their papers. One reporter, when asked by his Dayton hosts why he never attended trial sessions, replied, "Oh, I don't have to know what's going on; I know what my paper wants me to write."[13] A review of the trial press coverage reveals that the typical newsman had both an ear for a good story and a mouth hungry for Bryan's blood. Mencken, who had helped convince Darrow to break a lifelong rule and volunteer his services, advised him, "The thing to do is to make a fool out of Bryan."[14] Practicing what he preached, Mencken referred to Bryan as "the old mountebank," "old buzzard," and "a tinpot pope in the coca-cola belt."[15]

In addition to the obvious issues, there were others which stirred segments of the nation. Some people feared that Bryan would use Dayton as a springboard for a fourth try at the presidency — this time on a fundamentalist ticket. Others, remembering the ultimate triumph of Bryan's ideas regarding prohibition, the graduated income tax, woman suffrage, and direct election of U.S. Senators, feared a drive for a constitutional amend-

12 Paolo E. Coletta, *William Jennings Bryan III, Political Puritan, 1915–1925* (Lincoln, NE: University of Nebraska Press, 1969), p. 240.
13 Allem, *Backgrounds of the Scopes Trial*, p. 92.
14 Charles A. Fecher, *Mencken: A Study of His Thought* (New York: Knopf, distributed by Random House, 1978), p. 199.
15 Colletta, *William Jennings Bryan*, p. 256–257.

ment forbidding the teaching of evolution in tax-supported schools. That there was widespread interest in such a move was no fantasy, for the Tennessee evolution law was only 1 of 36 measures introduced in some 20 state legislatures in the 1920s.

Finally, the curtain for Act II rose on Friday, July 10, when the actual legal proceedings began two days after the 29th anniversary of Bryan's "Cross of Gold" speech. A stranger trial there probably never was. One or more of the jury were there primarily to get a good seat, but ironically they missed many proceedings because the jury was excluded from the lengthy, technical discussions.[16] Former colleagues and acquaintances were starred against each other. Darrow had campaigned for Bryan, Malone had served as Bryan's Undersecretary of State, and Scopes had been in the graduating class at Salem High School when Bryan gave the commencement address at his alma mater. Scientific experts were brought hundreds of miles to testify, but their statements were not accepted as evidence.[17]

Bryan addresses the court.

A worldwide audience followed the proceedings with keen interest, and critical responses sounded forth from such diverse

---

16 Allem, *Backgrounds of the Scopes Trial*, p. 76–77.

17 Although much has been made of the defense not being permitted to use the testimony of its scientists, disparaging acknowledgment has been given to the fact that the prosecution was also prepared to call on scientific experts. For example, on July 16, 1925, Bryan wrote to the famed Johns Hopkins University surgeon, Howard Kelly: "The court has excluded expert testimony, so we will not need to have you come. We have won every point so far and expect to win the suit." W. J. Bryan correspondence, Ac. No. 557, State Library and Archives, Nashville, Tennessee. See de Camp, *The Great Monkey Trial,* p. 125, for a defense "pseudo-scientist."

Foreground, left to right: Dudley Field Malone, Attorney General Stewart, W.J. Bryan, Judge Raulston, and Clarence Darrow.

individuals as George Bernard Shaw, Edgar Lee Masters, and Albert Einstein. The chief counsel for the defense (Darrow) was cited for contempt of court, and the leader for the prosecution (Bryan) took the witness stand. The accused never was called to testify. The defense, espousing the cause of science, as well as that of the ACLU, adopted the role of rhetorician by trying to establish the value of the theory of evolution; and the prosecution, espousing the cause of the state as well as that of biblical Christianity, adopted the role of dialectician by trying to establish that a law had been violated.[18] The proceedings were cut short by the judge partly to protect the chief prosecution and defense lawyers against threats on their safety.[19] The chief prosecutor (Bryan) did not feel the law involved should have had a penalty and consequently offered to pay Scopes' fine if he needed the money.[20]

When the climactic scene occurred in which Darrow cross-examined Bryan, only a half-dozen of the nearly two hundred newsmen were present. Scopes himself was pressed into service after the heated dialogue in order to help write up stories to cover things for the many members of the press who had inadvertently missed the hottest incident of the trial by stretching a lunch intermission into an afternoon search for a cool place to relax.[21]

Last in the list of trial oddities was the fact that the defense

---

18 Richard M. Weaver, *The Ethics of Rhetoric* (Chicago, IL: Regnery/Gateway Co., 1965), p. 30, 44–45.
19 de Camp, *The Great Monkey Trial*, p. 415.
   Coletta, *William Jennings Bryan*, p. 270.
20 de Camp, *The Great Monkey Trial*, p. 62–63, 126–127.
21 Scopes and Presley, *Center of the Storm*, p. 163, 183–184.

did not claim the accused was innocent of the charges, but at the end asked that the jury return a verdict of guilty.

Concerning the matter of Scopes' innocence, it is ironic that the defendant was never brought to the witness stand and asked the simple question on which the whole trial depended: Had he taught evolution? As Scopes later admitted, "To tell the truth, I wasn't sure I had taught evolution."[22] He was a coach, a mathematics, physics, chemistry, and general science teacher and had only briefly substituted as a biology teacher because of the regular teacher's illness. To prevent a possible cancellation of the court production, Scopes held a dress rehearsal in which he coached several of his students in the back of a taxi operated by "Stumpy" Reed (cousin to the "man-biting barber") as to what to say if called to the witness chair.[23]

Darrow addresses the jury.

In spite of all the ballyhoo, the trial involved serious, complex questions, and much of the court record portrayed skillful legal thrusting and parrying, not just by Bryan and Darrow but also by Arthur Garfield Hays, Dudley Field Malone, and Dr. John R. Neal for the defense and by Attorney General A. T. Stewart, William Jennings Bryan Jr., and Sue K. Hicks (the original "Boy Named Sue" of the Johnny Cash hit record) for the prosecution. The first six days were spent largely in such legal maneuverings as selection of a jury, questioning of the law's constitutionality, and debate over admissibility of expert testimony regarding evolution and the Bible. Two schoolboys, Howard Morgan and Harry Shelton, played supporting roles as witnesses on the fourth day.

The climax of interest and the beginning of Act III came on the seventh day, when Darrow was cited for contempt of court,

---

22 Ibid., p. 60.
23 Allem, *Backgrounds of the Scopes Trial*, p. 66.

and Bryan agreed to take the stand if he in turn would be allowed to cross-examine Darrow. Although the prosecution had tried to keep in center stage the legal issues of whether a law had been violated and whether the people had a right to control their own schools, Bryan, in his willingness to be a witness for biblical Christianity, opened himself to Darrow's scene-stealing tactics, which turned the spotlight on legally irrelevant issues, threw a bad light on the star prosecutor, and cast shadows on the law. Some of Darrow's questions were impossible for anyone to answer with factual certainty: Did the snake walk on his tail before God cursed him to crawl on his belly? Where did Cain get his wife? How old is the earth? How many people were there in Egypt and China 3,500–5,000 years ago?[24] Bryan's replies were a mixture of biblical knowledge, clever retorts, and frank admissions that he did not know some answers. They tended to portray him as a student of the Scriptures but not of science or ancient civilizations. Throughout the heated dialogue, Bryan emphasized what the biblical text actually said and forced Darrow to quote it rather than paraphrase it. The following is a fairly representative excerpt:

Q: But when you read that Jonah swallowed the whale — or that the whale swallowed Jonah — excuse me please — how do you literally interpret that?

A: When I read that a big fish swallowed Jonah — it does not say whale.

Q: Doesn't it? Are you sure?

A: That is my recollection of it. A big fish, and I believe it, and I believe in a God who can make a whale and can make a man and make both do what He pleases.

Q: Mr. Bryan, doesn't the New Testament say whale?

A: I am not sure. My impression is that it says fish; but it does not make so much difference; I merely called your attention to where it says fish — it does not say whale.

Q: But in the New Testament it says whale, doesn't it?

A: That may be true; I cannot remember in my own mind

---

24 Theodore C. Mercer, ed., *The World's Most Famous Court Trial: Tennessee Evolution Case* (1925; rpt. Dayton TN: Bryan College, 1978), p. 293–304. These questions were similar to ones Darrow had asked Bryan in a letter in the *Chicago Tribune*, July 4, 1923, according to Ray Ginger, *Six Days or Forever? Tennessee v. John Thomas Scopes* (New York: New American Library, 1958), p. 33.

what I read about it.

Q: Now, you say, the big fish swallowed Jonah, and he there remained how long — three days — and then he spewed him upon the land. You believe that the big fish was made to swallow Jonah?

A: I am not prepared to say that; the Bible merely says it was done.

Q: You don't know whether it was the ordinary run of fish, or made for that purpose?

A: You may guess; you evolutionists guess.

Q: But when we do guess, we have a sense to guess right.

A: But do not do it often.

Q: You are not prepared to say whether that fish was made especially to swallow a man or not?

A: The Bible doesn't say, so I am not prepared to say.

Q: You don't know whether that was fixed up specially for the purpose.

A: No, the Bible doesn't say.

Q: But you do believe He made them — that He made such a fish and that it was big enough to swallow Jonah?

A: Yes, sir. Let me add: One miracle is just as easy to believe as another.

Q: It is for me.

A: It is for me.

Q: Just as hard?

A: It is hard to believe for you, but easy for me. A miracle is a thing performed beyond what man can perform. When you get beyond what man can do, you get within the realm of miracles; and it is just as easy to believe the miracle of Jonah as any other miracle in the Bible.

Q: Perfectly easy to believe that Jonah swallowed the whale?

A: If the Bible said so; the Bible doesn't make as extreme statements as evolutionists do.[25]

Early in the questioning, Bryan avoided being trapped by Darrow into a hyperliteralist corner by stating that he believed "everything in the Bible should be accepted as it is given there," but he recognized that "some of the Bible is given illustratively,"

---

25 Mercer, *The World's Most Famous Court Trial*, p. 285.

John T. Scopes arraigned.

and such figurative language should be interpreted accordingly. Later he acknowledged that he did not believe the days of creation were necessarily 24-hour days, because the word for *day* was used in Genesis 2:4 to mean a period of time. This position, which Bryan probably believed to be biblically broad-minded and semantically sound, was misinterpreted by the defense and then broadened to mean "that these things are not to be taken literally, but that each man is entitled to his own interpretation."[26]

On the eighth and final day, Bryan and Darrow's lengthy repartee was expunged from the record as not being germane. Darrow, realizing that he could not win the case as long as the prosecution stuck to the main issue, asked the judge to instruct the jury to find Scopes guilty. This move upstaged Bryan by preventing him from putting Darrow on the stand and from delivering his final speech; in addition, it provided for the case to be taken to a higher court where philosophical issues could be debated. Having begun with a bang, the trial ended with a whimper on July 21, when Scopes was found guilty and fined $100. The Tennessee Supreme Court later upheld the constitutionality of the law but reversed Scopes' conviction on the technicality that the jury — not the judge — should have set the fine.

During the five days following the trial, most of the principals returned home. But Bryan, in spite of doctors' warnings about his weak heart and diabetic condition, prepared for publication the 15,000-word monologue which he had not been allowed to deliver when Judge John T. Raulston brought the trial to a sud-

26 Ibid., p. 285, 298–302.

den conclusion. In addition, the "Great Commoner" hiked around the rugged Dayton countryside with a local committee looking at possible sites for a school that he had suggested be built. Then, narrowly escaping possible death when an auto nicked him on the left side, he traveled several hundred miles over rough 1925 Tennessee roads to speak, to consult with Chattanooga printers, to read proofs of his last message, and to have a medical check on his diabetes. He delivered an address at Jasper before a crowd of 2,000, orated for two hours in the broiling sun at a fair in Winchester, and spoke to approximately 50,000 people along the return trip to Chattanooga.

On Sunday, July 26, Bryan drove to Dayton and participated in the morning worship service of the Southern Methodist Church. That afternoon he died quietly in his sleep. Five days later in Arlington National Cemetery, his body was laid to rest beneath the inscription, "He Kept the Faith." It was raining heavily, but just as the casket was being lowered out of sight, the dark clouds parted momentarily to disclose a rainbow.[27] Bryan's passing marked the end of the final act of the legal drama, but the beginning of an epilogue which shows no signs of concluding.

In less than three months after Bryan's death, friends from all over the country joined with "Hustling Druggist" F.E. Robinson and other citizens of Dayton in initiating a memorial university to honor Bryan's life and his desire that a school be established on one of the hills surrounding Dayton. Governor Victor Donahey of Ohio, Governor Austin Peay of Tennessee, and other dignitaries served on the National Campaign Committee. In spite of the crushing blow of the Great Depression, which forced cancellation of more than half of the approximately one million dollars pledged for the school, the doors were opened in 1930 in the old high school building where John T. Scopes had supposedly taught evolution.

During the 13 years that Bryan's great antagonist, Darrow, lived after the trial, he returned to Dayton on one occasion and noticed that across the street from Robinson's Drugstore workmen were constructing a new building for the Cumberland Presbyterian Church, a denomination with which Bryan, Scopes, Robinson, and trial juror Jess Goodrich all had associations. Darrow quipped, "I guess I didn't do much good here after all."[28]

27 Coletta, *William Jennings Bryan*, p. 271–276.
28 de Camp, *The Great Monkey Trial*, p. 492.

Promoter George Rappleyea moved away to try out for other ventures. In Cuba he worked on an anti-mildew roofing process, and in Canada he developed extra-hard airstrip paving made from blackstrap molasses.[29] Silent star Scopes, who had become the forgotten man in the whole production, left Dayton, studied geology at the University of Chicago, worked for an oil company in Venezuela for several years, and finally moved to Louisiana, where he was employed by a gas company. He died in 1970, three years after Rappleyea.

After the closing curtain of the trial, Dayton continued to

Joe Mendi — the chimpanzee.

grow, turning a deaf ear to jeering ridicule so severe that it even affected the Nashville circle of fugitive poets and agrarian critics, serving "like a midnight alarm" to the experimentation of the former[30] and acting as "the one event which undoubtedly did most to engage the [latter] in religious polemics."[31] It made members such as John Crowe Ransom wary of the trend to deify science and concerned for the defense of fundamentalism.[32] The moniker of "Monkey Town," assigned to Dayton for its Scopes trial publicity stunt, has not discouraged area residents from enthusiastically promoting such annual endeavors as the East Tennessee Strawberry Festival, which attracts over 20,000 people, and the March of Dimes Drive, in which Rhea County led the nation in 1972 in dollars-per-capita giving. Dayton's development includes diversified industries representing divisions of several national corporations, an extensive urban renewal project, over a score of areas for middle-to-upper-middle-class homes as well as a hospital-rest

29 Telephone interview with Juanita Corvin Tennyson, May 25, 1977.
30 Donald Davidson, "The Thankless Muse and Her Fugitive Poets," *Sewanee Review,* 67, Spring 1958, p. 228.
31 Alexander Karanikas, *Tillers of a Myth: Southern Agrarians as Social and Literary Critics* (Madison, WI: University of Wisconsin Press, 1969), p. 145.
32 Louise Cowan, *The Fugitive Group: A Literary History* (Baton Rouge, LA: Louisiana State University Press, 1959), p. 245.

home complex, an airport, two radio stations, two shopping centers, an award-winning consolidated high school (replacing the one in which Scopes taught), and an elementary school whose students have ranked first, second, and fourth in recent years on tests in a statewide evaluation program.

Although the promoters of the trial got the publicity but not the major industry they hoped for at the time, in the north end of Rhea County a one-and-one-half-billion-dollar nuclear power plant has been constructed about 20 miles from the Scopes trial courthouse, and this promises to open the door for much industrial growth. The town's record of physical growth is contrary to the reports of some journalists, whose theme song about Dayton has been, to quote one wire story, "Not much has changed here in the last half-century."[33]

There is a William Jennings Bryan College, contrary to the accounts of several writers. Some have played down references to it,[34] omitted any references to it in a description of present-day Dayton,[35] claimed that it was "still born,"[36] or suggested its non-existence by stating that except for the historical marker at the courthouse, "There is little external evidence that in this town one of the most extraordinary legal and social spectacles of the twentieth century United States riveted the attention of the country and much of the world for 12 days one sweltering July."[37]

Bryan College is an institution of about 500 students from some 30 states and 10 foreign countries, and it has a 100-acre campus of 11 major buildings and several auxiliary structures. The college is an accredited, coeducational institution emphasizing the liberal arts from an evangelical Christian perspective. In its Bible, science, and related courses, it endeavors to examine the evidence attending human theories of evolution

---

33 Dee Siegelbaum, "Better Not Monkey Around with Evolution in Dayton," *Times-Union and Journal* [Jacksonville, Fla.], June 9, 1974, Sec. I, p. 6. See also Carlyle Marney's comment: "There wasn't anything at Dayton then (1789) and there isn't too much now." "Dayton's Long Hot Summer," *D-Days at Dayton: Reflections on the Scopes Trial*, ed. Jerry R. Tompkins (Baton Rouge, LA: Louisiana State University Press, 1965), p. 133.

34 In his 224-page book, Ray Ginger devotes only two paragraphs to the institution: one to plans for founding it and one emphasizing such problems as low economic status and enrollment prior to 1941. *Six Days or Forever?* p. 123, 186.

35 "Stop on Highway 27 — Monkey Trial Town Today," *Newsweek*, Sept. 1, 1958, p. 35.

36 Marney, "Dayton's Long Hot Summer," 133.

37 Boyce Rensberger, " 'Monkey Trial' is 50 Years Old," *New York Times*, July 10, 1975, Sec. C, p. 58.

and various interpretations of the biblical record of creation, teaching students to search for truth not only in the Bible but also in the biology laboratory. Mindful of the fact that William Jennings Bryan and the Fundamentalists were criticized for supposedly refusing to tolerate more than a single interpretation of man's origins, the college has sought to maintain a spirit of open inquiry without compromising its biblical heritage.

The accusation of intolerance leveled at William Jennings Bryan tended to disregard the published record of his statements, some of which were made several years before the trial and others immediately after it. In his address to the Constitutional Convention of Nebraska in 1920, Bryan said, "We do not ask public school teachers to teach religion in the schools, and teachers, paid by taxation, should not be permitted to attack our Bible in the schools." Three years later he wrote, "Christians do not ask that the teachers in the public schools, colleges, and universities become exponents of orthodox Christianity . . . but Christians have a right to protest against teaching that weakens faith in God, undermines belief in the Bible, and reduces Christ to the stature of a man."

Bryan suggested that since Christians build their own schools when they want to teach their doctrines, evolutionists should do the same for promulgating theirs. Again in 1923, Bryan wrote to Senator W.J. Singleterry, urging that the Florida legislature attach no penalty to its proposed anti-evolution law and that the law prohibit only the teaching of evolution as a fact, for "a book which merely contains it as an hypothesis can be considered as giving information as to views held, which is very different from teaching it as a fact."[38]

Though often caricatured as an anti-intellectual who was afraid of the truth if it did not agree with his beliefs, Bryan, who was a member of the American Society for the Advancement of Science,[39] remarked to C.H. Thurber in 1923, "It is not the facts that do harm"; rather it is the "forced conclusions unsupported by fact." Evolution, therefore, "should be considered with an open mind" and its statements "fairly weighed."

"All truth is of God," Bryan argued in the August 1923

---

38 Lawrence W. Levine, *Defender of the Faith: William Jennings Bryan: The Last Decade, 1915–1925* (New York: Oxford University Press, 1965), p. 263, 278–279, 285–286.

39 Coletta, *William Jennings Bryan*, p. 230, footnote.

issue of *Popular Science Monthly*, "whether found in the book of nature or in the Book of Books; but guesses are not science; hypotheses such as the hypothesis of evolution are not truths."[40]

Did Bryan's idealism evaporate under the heat of the realistic pressures associated with the trial? In a letter dated May 28, 1925, Bryan wrote to Dayton lawyer Sue K. Hicks: "The *right* of the *people* speaking through the legislature, to control the schools which they *create* and *support* is the real issue" (emphasis his).[41] Bryan carefully maintained this position during the trial period, when he re-affirmed on Sunday, July 12, "There is no attack on free speech, or freedom of the press, or freedom of thought, or freedom of knowledge, but surely parents have a right to guard the religious welfare of their children."[42]

After the trial, Bryan and his wife discussed the matter of intolerance on their way to Winchester from a speaking engagement in Jasper. Mrs. Bryan records the conversation:

> We spoke of . . . an encroachment on individual religious belief which is a sacred domain. We agreed that care must be taken at this point that no religious zeal should invade this sacred domain and become intolerance.
>
> Mr. Bryan said, "Well, Mamma, I have not made that mistake yet, have I?" And I replied, "You are all right so far, but will you be able to keep to this narrow path?" With a happy smile, he said, "I think I can." "But," said I, "can you control your followers?" and more gravely he said, "I think I can." And I knew he was adding mentally, "by the help of God."[43]

Bryan had already arrived at this conclusion earlier when he wrote to C.L. Ficklin, "The collective right is bound to protect itself from misrepresentation and is just as sacred as the individual's right to think for himself as an individual."[44]

40 Willard H. Smith, *The Social and Religious Thought of William Jennings Bryan* (Lawrence, KA: Coronado Press, 1975), p. 183–184.

41 de Camp, *The Great Monkey Trial*, p. 126–127.

42 Louis W. Koenig, *Bryan: A Political Biography of William Jennings Bryan* (New York: Putnam, 1971), p. 641.

43 William Jennings Bryan and Mary Baird Bryan, *The Memoirs of William Jennings Bryan* (Philadelphia, PA: John C. Winston Co., 1925), p. 485–486.

44 Koenig, *Bryan: A Political Biography*, p. 631.

As John Crowe Ransom noted concerning the Scopes trial, and as scholars have since discussed, below the questions of collective versus individual rights, evolution versus religion, and academic freedom versus parental concerns; below the economic exigencies prompting the publicity stunt of the trial; below the machinations of the press, helping to promote the trial; below all these lay the modernist-fundamentalist conflict of the period.[45] This controversy, whose stage was the battle over the nature of the Bible, produced a whole cycle of dramatic confrontations, of which the Scopes trial was but one. Bryan and Darrow played roles which were somewhat representative of the other protagonists and antagonists in the controversy, but each did so in his own characteristic manner.

Though years ahead of his time in his liberal and progressive ideas concerning political and social action, Bryan was a biblical conservative in religion.[46] With the fundamentalists, he shared beliefs in the divine inspiration and authority of the Scriptures; the deity, virgin birth, miracles, and physical resurrection of Christ; and the efficacy of Christ's substitutionary death on the cross for the sins of mankind.[47] Such positions led Bryan to take a stance which tended toward absolutist authoritarianism in matters of morality and religion, which emphasized the importance of spiritual values in all aspects of life, and which viewed the evolutionary hypothesis as a challenge to the authority of God — the foundation for the Bible, Christianity, and ultimately all of civilization.[48]

---

45 John Crowe Ransom, *God Without Thunder: An Unorthodox Defense of Orthodoxy* (Hamden, CN: Harcourt, Brace & Co., 1930 rpt.; Archon Books, 1965), p. 4–6, 98–101, et passim.

de Camp, *The Great Monkey Trial*, p. 24–56.

Allem, *Backgrounds of the Scopes Trial*, p. 31–40.

Ginger, *Six Days or Forever?* p. 13–21, 29–34.

46 Coletta, *William Jennings Bryan*, p. 298.

Koenig, *Bryan: A Political Biography*, p. 12.

Henry S. Commager, "William Jennings Bryan," *William Jennings Bryan and the Campaign of 1896*, ed. George F. Whicher (Boston, MA: Raytheon Education Co./Heath, 1953), p. 88.

47 David F. Wells and John D. Woodbridge, eds., *The Evangelicals: What They Believe, Who They Are, Where They Are Changing* (New York: Abingdon Press, 1975), p. 30, 173.

William Jennings Bryan, *Seven Questions in Dispute* (Philadelphia, PA: Fleming H. Revell Co., 1924). Bryan devotes a chapter to each of the fundamental beliefs noted above.

48 Ginger, *Six Days or Forever?* p. 16–17, 34, 203.

Bryan, *Seven Questions in Dispute*, p. 151, 157–158.

Rhea County Courthouse — scene
of Scopes evolution trial.

Darrow, on the other
hand, put his faith in doubt
and inquiry rather than in
God, and his trust was in
reason rather than in revelation. To him, the Bible was
to be accepted as any other
book.[49] Darrow's outlook
on man led him to cham-
pion the individual over the
majority, hence his defense
of Scopes. For some time
before the trial, Darrow had found Bryan's opinions dangerous;
consequently, he saw the trial as an opportunity to expose and
refute them.[50] On the last day of the trial, Darrow said in his
closing remarks, "I think this case will be remembered because
it is the first case of this sort since we stopped trying people in
America for witchcraft, because here we have done our best to
turn back the tide that has sought to force itself upon this —
upon this modern world, of testing every fact in science by a
religious dictum."[51]

In addition to the Rhea County Courthouse restoration and
Scopes Trial Museum project, the epilogue to the trial has included since 1988 a July Scopes Trial Festival, which features
Destiny in Dayton, a documentary play based almost entirely on
the transcript of the trial. For the more serious students of the
entire event, Bryan College makes available more than 20 publi-
cations, including a reprint of the first book published on the
trial, *The World's Most Famous Court Trial.* This edition contains a transcript of the trial; relevant legal documents; updated
historical information; annotated bibliographies of the trial, creationism, and evolution; and William Jennings Bryan's 15,000-
word culminating speech, which was undelivered when the court

---

49 See Darrow's answers to Bryan's questions, de Camp, *The Great Monkey Trial,* p.
   428–431.
   Ginger, *Six Days or Forever?* p. 57.
50 Ibid., p. 33.
51 Mercer, *The World's Most Famous Court Trial,* p. 317.

proceedings were cut short. In spite of the fact that some reporters and researchers have wearied the people of Dayton by their misleading accounts, most visitors have encountered a friendly reception from such people as F.E. Robinson's children, Frances and Sonny, or former County Judge Daisy Morgan, in whose home Scopes was a frequent guest. But the visitor who tries to create a comic scene at the expense of the local citizens by asking if any monkeys live in Dayton, may find himself upstaged by Mrs. Morgan's repartee: "No monkeys live here, but quite a few pass through."[52]

---

52 Personal interview with Daisy Morgan, July 9, 1976.

CHAPTER 2

MR. BRYAN ON EVOLUTION

by William Jennings Bryan

"He being dead yet speaketh" (Heb. 11:4). The "Great Commoner," William Jennings Bryan, died over 70 years ago, but he was undoubtedly the most widely known creationist of his generation. The following article, first published in August 1925, soon after the famous Scopes trial, was written by him shortly before his death, and we believe it should still be read today.

Are those who reject evolution as an unproved hypothesis *unreasonable* in refusing to accept, as conclusive, the evidence offered by evolutionists in support of a proposition that links every living thing in blood relationship to every other living thing — the rose to the onion, the eagle to the mosquito, the mockingbird to the rattlesnake, the royal palm to the scrub oak, and man to all? Surely, so astounding a proposition should be supported by facts before it becomes binding upon the judgment of a rational being.

It is not unusual for evolutionists to declare that their hypothesis is as clearly established as the law of gravitation

William Jennings Bryan

or the roundness of the earth. Yet anyone can prove that anything heavier than air, when thrown up into the air, will fall to the ground; anyone can demonstrate the roundness of the earth by traveling around it.

But how about the doctrine that all of the species (Darwin estimated the number at from two to three million — the lowest estimate is one million, about a half-million of which have been tabulated) by the operation of interior, resident forces came by slow and gradual development from one or a few germs of life, which appeared on this planet millions of years ago — the estimates varying according to the vigor of the guesser's imagination and the number of ciphers he has left in his basket? Can that proposition be demonstrated by everyone like the law of gravitation or the roundness of the earth? On the contrary, no one has ever been able to trace one single species to another. Darwin admitted that no species had ever been traced to another, but he thought his hypothesis should be accepted even though the "missing links" had not been found. He did not say link, as some seem to think, but *links*. If there is such a thing as evolution, it is not just one link — the link between man and the lower forms of life — that is missing, but all the millions of links between millions of species. Our case is even stronger; it has been pointed out that evolution, if there is such a force, would act so *slowly* that there would be an infinite number of links between each two species; or a million times a million links in all, every one of which is missing.

Thomas Huxley also asserted that no species had ever been traced to another; and, while a friend of Darwin, declared that until some species could be traced to another, Darwin's hypothesis did not rise to the dignity of a theory. Prof. William Bateson (a London biologist, prominent enough to be invited to cross the Atlantic and speak to the members of the American Society for the Advancement of Science), at Toronto two years ago last December, in discussing evolution, took up every effort that had been made to discover the origin of species, and declared that every one had failed — every one! Yet he still asserted faith in evolution, showing how much easier it is for some scientists to have faith along their own line of work than along religious lines.

Why should we believe that *all* species come one from another when no evidence has yet been found to prove that *any* species came from another? If evolution were true, every square foot of the earth's surface would teem with conclusive proof of change. The entire absence of proof is the strongest possible proof that evolution is a myth.

But those who reject evolution have another proof. Chemistry refutes all the claims of the evolutionists, and proves that there is no pushing power to be found anywhere in nature — no progressive force at work in the earth — no eternal urge lifting matter or life from any plane to a higher one. Chemistry has failed to find any trace of force active enough to raise life, step by step, up along the lines of the family tree imagined by Darwin, from "a group of marine animals, resembling the larvae of existing ascidians" to "man, the wonder and glory of the universe."

On the contrary, the only active force discovered on the planet as pointed out by Edwin Slosson, is deterioration, decay, death. All the formulae of chemistry are exact and permanent. They leave no room for the guesses upon which evolutionists build other guesses, *ad infinitum*. Take water, for instance; it must have been on earth before any living thing appeared, because it is the daily need of every living thing. And it has been H_2O from the beginning. Every one of the millions of changes of species imagined by the evolutionists have taken place — if they have taken place at all — since water came upon the earth. But water has not changed; neither has anything else ever changed, so far as nature has revealed her processes to man.

When a few bones and a piece of skull are fashioned into a supposed likeness of a prehistoric animal, described as an ape-man, the evolutionists fall down before it and worship it, although it contains a smaller percentage of fact than the one-half percent alcohol permitted in a legal beverage. . . . Someone searching for fossils in a sand hill in Nebraska came upon a lonely tooth. The body of the animal had disappeared; not even a jaw bone survived. Professor Osborn summoned a few congenial spirits, nearly as credulous as himself, and they held a post mortem examination on this insignificant tooth. After due deliberation, they announced that the tooth was the long-looked-for missing link which the world awaited.

Give science a fact and it is invincible. But no one can guess more wildly than a scientist, when he has no compass but his imagination, and no purpose but to get away from God. Darwin uses the phrase "we may well suppose" 800 times and wins for himself a high place among the unconscious humorists by his efforts to explain things that are not true. For instance, he assumed that man has a brain superior to woman's brain, and tried to explain it on the theory that our ancestors were brutes and that the males, fighting for female mates, increased their brain power. He also assumed that our ancestors were hairy animals, and tried to explain the disappearance of the hair on the theory that the females selected their companions and, because of a universal preference, selected the least hairy and thus, in the course of ages, bred the hair off. The two explanations would be funny enough, even if each did not make the other impossible — the two sexes could not do the selecting at the same time.

Evolutionists also explain to us that light, beating on the skin, brought out the eye, although the explanation does not tell us why the light waves did not continue to beat until they brought out eyes all over the body. They also tell us that the leg is a development from a wart that accidentally appeared on the belly of a legless animal; and that we dream of falling because our ancestors fell out of trees 50,000 years ago.

It is a calamity that highly educated men should while away their time in idle speculation instead of devoting themselves to the serious problems that demand solution.

Editor's Addendum

The foregoing article was first published in the *Reader's Digest* in August 1925 (vol. 4, no. 40), less than three years after the *Digest* first began publication. At that time, the magazine was not as strongly committed to evolutionism as it is today (the editors have adamantly refused to publish creationist articles in recent years).

The article is of particular interest as a brief summary of some of the anti-evolution arguments of 70 years ago — arguments that, for the most part, are as cogent today as they were then.

It is interesting to note Mr. Bryan's sarcastic critique of the famous tooth which Henry Fairfield Osborn, Director of the American Museum of Natural History, had publicized far and wide as the ancient "Nebraska Man." Mr. Bryan died shortly before the discovery of a more complete skeleton of the creature, revealing it to have been not an ape-man (nor an ape, nor a man!) but an extinct pig!

Mr. Bryan also noted the significance of the universal law of deterioration. Modern creationists frequently use this same cogent evidence, although it is more accurately known as the law of entropy.

William Jennings Bryan, of course, was the most famous creationist of his day. Although he was not a scientist, his political eminence and oratorical ability impelled him into that role. He was born in 1860, so was 65 at the time of the Scopes trial. He had been the Democratic candidate for president in 1896, 1900, and 1908, but was defeated each time, although known as one of the finest public speakers who ever lived. He was called "The Great Commoner." He served as Secretary of State under President Woodrow Wilson from 1912 to 1915.

Spiritually, he was a Presbyterian, and became an opponent of evolution after realizing the great war (World War I) was a direct outgrowth of evolutionary teaching in Germany, and that evolutionary teaching in American public schools and colleges was contributing significantly to the decline of morals and Christianity in general.

On the other hand, he was not a young-earth creationist, even advocating progressive creationism while being questioned by the ACLU attorney, Clarence Darrow, on the witness stand at the Scopes trial. This compromise, which is widespread today among evangelicals, earned him no sympathy, however, from either Darrow or the liberal press. The very fact that he believed in God and the Bible was sufficient, in their view, to subject him to ridicule.

Nevertheless, the points made in his *Digest* article, and in the much longer declamation he had prepared (but was maneuvered out of giving by Darrow and the trial judge) for his trial summary, constitute a strong case against evolution even today.

For Further Reading

William Jennings Bryan, *The Last Message of William Jennings Bryan* (Dayton, TN: Bryan College, 1975).

CHAPTER 3

THE DAYTON DECEPTION

by John D. Morris

The Scopes trial can only be fully comprehended within a larger framework — the long war against God. Only when we see the creation/evolution conflict[1] as the collision of two world views can we understand the utter hatred toward Christianity on display at the Scopes trial.

Even though John Scopes was "convicted" of teaching evolution, in many ways the anti-creationists won a major victory. During the trial, Christians were depicted as ignorant, foolish anti-intellectuals. And this image was portrayed to the world by the media, since "to the victor belongs the spoils." Evolutionists are still enjoying the incredible gains they made through the Scopes trial, in society, in the courts, in politics — even in religious circles. Evolution has become known as "the central unifying concept" for all rational discussion. Creation, and to a large degree Christianity, has been ridiculed, ignored, or legislated out of the public arena.

A Look at the Two World Views

The main difference between the two world views is in the origin of life. Creation, on its face, presupposes a supernatural origin of all things, and a spiritual understanding of nature. There is no such thing as creation without a Creator. Acts of creation cannot be observed today, but by observing those things which do exist, creationists conclude life could not have come about by

---

1 Henry M. Morris, *The Long War Against God: The History and Impact of the Creation/Evolution Conflict* (Grand Rapids, MI: Baker Book House, 1989).

natural processes, but only by supernatural processes.

Evolution, at its core, is an attempt to understand all things as natural phenomena — the random, chance results of natural processes. Most evolutionists admit that evolution, in any meaningful sense, goes too slowly to observe, if it still occurs at all. Thus, it too is an idea about the nature of the unobserved past. This view colors every observation and reconstruction of history. Only natural processes are allowed, and the supernatural is excluded.

Obviously, both naturalism and supernaturalism are religious faith positions. The question, then, becomes: Which religious bias is the correct one? Since neither can be observed, the best we can do is to see which view of history fits the observable facts best, and that is the one that is more likely correct.

Let us briefly look at some major scientific observations. Consider the unimaginable complexity in living things. The complexity of even the simplest single-celled organism dwarfs that of the largest man-made computer. Evolutionists think simple life originated from non-living chemicals — all by chance. Yet this life is far too complex for man to understand, let alone duplicate. If computers do not happen by chance, is it really credible to think that life, which is profoundly more complex, could generate spontaneously by chance?[2]

When organisms reproduce today, their offspring resemble their parents. No evidence exists to suggest that these organisms change into something else. Darwin proposed that the process of

2 Charles B. Thaxton, Walter L. Bradley, and Roger L. Olsen, *The Mystery of Life's Origin*, 4th ed. (Dallas, TX: Lewis & Stanley, 1992).

natural selection accomplished evolutionary changes. Later on, mutations were thought to produce the genetic material. But surprisingly, not one new and different species has ever been produced by natural selection, as far as observational science knows. Natural selection works, but it just does not produce anything new. It works to conserve what already exists, and weed out any misfits. No mutation — not one truly beneficial or positive mutation — has ever been observed. While a few mutations have produced a trait in a plant or animal that was preferred by man, these changes have been harmful to the organism itself in a natural sense. Mutations should rightly be called birth defects. They will not produce positive evolutionary changes.[3]

Today biologists speak of beneficial recombination of genes or some other factor, but at best all that is produced is a variety of a living type. The ultimate question is: How did the organism itself arise? Better yet, from where did the original genetic code arise, and who coded it to contain such a wealth of information?

Leaders in evolutionary thought now argue that they are still searching for the mechanism of evolution, because all ideas proposed in the past have been shown to be impotent. A theory that claims to be responsible for everything that exists, and does not even have a mechanism, is weak indeed.

The weakest link in the evolutionary chain is the origin of life from non-life. If anything is impossible, this is it. The problem here is so serious that some evolutionists have adopted the concept of "panspermia." Since life could not have arisen here on earth, it must have happened somewhere else, they say, out in outer space where the conditions were different and perhaps natural laws were different, coming here perhaps on a meteoroid. Some hold to this ridiculous idea, and yet claim that the origin of life could never have been the result of a supernatural Creator.

Surely, if evolution occurred over billions of years it would be recorded in the fossil record. We should see evidence that some basic types of organisms have changed into others. Such transitions may have taken millions of years, and we should be able to find some of the transitional, or in-between forms. Darwin was frustrated by the lack of clear examples in his day, but predicted that many would soon be found. However, as of today viable transitional fossil forms have not been uncovered. In the

---

3 Pierre P. Grassé, *Evolution of Living Organisms* (New York: Academic Press, 1977).

1970s, evolutionists began to admit the lack of evolutionary transitions in the fossil record,[4] and set about modifying the evolutionary theory to fit. Now, many teach that organisms remain the same for long periods of time, and then evolve so rapidly that they leave no fossils.

The two biggest gaps in the fossil record prove the point. Even if single-celled organisms did exist, how did they evolve into the vast array of ocean-bottom-dwelling invertebrates? This is called the Cambrian explosion — an explosion of life that has baffled evolutionists.[5] Suddenly clams, snails, brachiopods, corals, starfish, jellyfish, trilobites, and many other organisms appear in the fossil record with *no* ancestors at all. The transition is thought to have taken some three billion years, yet not one transitional form has been found!

The next biggest gap in the fossil record is from marine invertebrates to vertebrate fish. Was a clam or a jellyfish the ancestor of fish? This transition is thought to have taken tens of millions of years. Again, nothing has been found which serves as a plausible ancestor for the fish.

If evolution cannot climb over these two hurdles, we can consider it to be, pardon the pun, dead in the water.

Changes are seen. People in America are taller on the average than they were 2,000 years ago. But that is not evolution; it is due to better nutrition and medical care. Grasshopper populations grow resistant to DDT,[6] but that is not evolution. A small percentage of grasshoppers have always been resistant to DDT, and the non-resistant ones have been killed without leaving offspring. The predominantly light variety of peppered moths in England was replaced by a darker variety during the smoggy industrial revolution. But that is not evolution; it was the same moth before and after, with differing proportions of dark and light moths alive at the time. This might be natural selection, but not evolution; nothing new was produced.[7] Small changes within a species (which *are* observed) do not prove the big changes into

---

4 Duane T. Gish, *Evolution: The Fossils Still Say No!* (El Cajon, California: Institute for Creation Research, 1995).

5 J.H. Lipps and P.W. Signor, eds., *Origin and Early Evolution of the Metazoa* (New York: Plenum Press, 1982).

6 Francisco Ayala, "The Mechanisms of Evolution," *Scientific American*, vol. 239, September 1978, p. 63.

7 Michael Denton, *Evolution: A Theory in Crisis* (Bethesda, MD: Adler & Adler Publishers, Inc., 1986; Great Britain: Burnett Books Ltd., 1985).

new types (which are not observed), no matter how often our evolutionary colleagues insist that it does. All the changes that we observe are variations within a species. There is no leaping from species to species — all changes occur within the boundaries of species. Evolutionists should not just guess how evolution might have occurred: they should show that it did occur, and was responsible for life and its vast array of living forms.

In many ways, natural selection provides a barrier to evolution. If the forelimb of a walking reptile transformed into the wing of a bird, each evolutionary step would have to provide some advantage over its predecessor and thus be "selected" by nature (natural selection) for survival. But long before the forelimb was a good wing, with feathers rather than scales, hollow bones in place of solid, warm-blooded instead of cold-blooded, and so on, it would be a terrible leg and eliminated by natural selection. What benefit is half a wing?

To top it all off, even the basic laws of science forbid evolution. In particular, the "Second Law of Science," which has never been violated in all of observational science, shows that in any process the disorder of a system tends to increase.[8] We know this to be true as we see

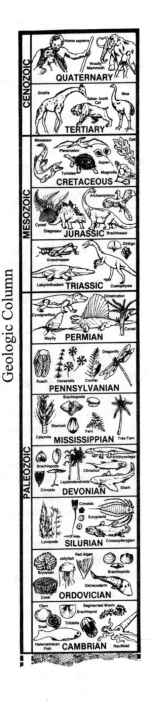

Geologic Column

---

8 Isaac Asimov, "In the Game of Energy and Thermodynamics You Can't Even Break Even," *Smithsonian Institute Journal,* June 1970, p. 4–10.

things grow old, wear out, decay, and die.

Everything goes downhill, but evolutionists insist things have become more complex over time. They claim the law can be overcome by providing extra energy from the sun. However, the more uncontrolled energy is added, the faster the system runs downhill. In order to build up in complexity, there must be a way to convert the incoming energy into useful forms. Solar energy, for example, is converted by photosynthesis into useful forms, and applied in specific ways through the DNA code in the plant seed. These features must pre-exist the energy, or the plant will die. The growth which does result is not evolution. No new genetic material was formed at all. Evolution is against this basic law of science.

The Evidence in 1925

If evolution is not well-supported now, consider its state at the time of the Scopes trial. Evolution had become rather popular among intellectuals, as is also true today, but a look at the scientific evidence presented reveals just how weak the case was.

The evidence had a particular slant. At stake was not just the theory of evolution; it was that men had evolved from ape-like creatures. Almost all lines of evidence attempted to link man with the animals. Very little evidence for evolution was presented, but every possible argument for human evolution found its way into the trial and the media coverage surrounding the trial.

As we look back on this evidence *now*, we recognize that every argument presented for evolution at the Scopes trial has been disproved. Two arguments from biology were aired, and four examples of supposed ape-men made their appearance. In each case, the arguments are no longer valid. Let us look briefly at each one.

Vestigial Organs

In the early 1900s, some scientists claimed that a number of human body parts were non-functional — such as the appendix or the tonsils — and they were thought to be useless leftovers from evolutionary ancestors. Such organs may have had a use in the past, they reasoned, but evolution had made them invalid. The useless leftovers were labeled "vestigial."

But in reality, what does this show? Does this really mean that the organs, muscles, or glands have no function, or only that medical science has not yet discovered the function? As it turns out, the latter is correct. Uses for one after the other have been found. The list has decreased from almost 200 useless organs to zero.

It is true that some parts may not be necessary, but does this mean they are useless? We can live without a hand or a leg, but retaining them is preferable. Many people have had their tonsils or appendix removed, and suffer little. But it is now known that each plays a role in the body's immune system.[9] It is better to keep these organs, even though one can live without them.

Some organs only contribute under extreme circumstances which are seldom faced, but their lack can prove deadly. A recent study in Japan showed that those who had their appendix survived radiation poisoning at a much higher rate than those without an appendix.

Some organs play an important role during infancy or even in the womb, only to become rather inoperative later in life. Without their early function, however, life would have ceased.

Today's scientists are following a similar route. By studying life's genetic code, scientists have observed that much of the DNA strand of coded information remains idle. Ten years ago scientists came to regard this "junk DNA" as evolution leftovers. But now[10] several functions have been discovered; some operate as back-up, replacing damaged "working" parts; some provide a template to ensure accurate copying during reproduction; other sections provide three-dimensional spacing in the DNA coiled helix that is necessary for proper function; many sections operate during fetal development but not afterwards; and the functions for still others are just now being discovered. God's design of the human body and its myriad interdependent parts is exquisite.

Scientists need to learn humility from the lesson of vestigial organs. Only the height of arrogance would lead a fallible

---

9 S.R. Scadding, "Do 'Vestigial Organs' Provide Evidence for Evolution?" *Evolution Theory*, vol. 5, May 1981, p. 173–176. A rebuttal by Bruce G. Naylor appeared in the September 1982 issue and a reply by the author in the December 1981 issue.
10 Philip Yam, "Talking Trash," *Scientific American*, vol. 23, March 1995, p. 45.

scientist, operating from lack of data and understanding, to pass judgment on God's design. How much better to acknowledge one's own inadequacies and adopt a wait-and-see attitude toward the mysteries which remain.

Embryonic Recapitulation

Once Darwin's book was published, it gathered a strange gallery of followers, but none more dubious than Ernst Haeckel. A German biologist, he championed Darwin's theories on the European continent, much as Huxley did in England. Ideas of naturalism, racism, and imperialism were already gaining in popularity in Germany, and Darwin's views — survival of the fittest, might makes right, and elimination of the less fit — provided the fertile seed-bed for national socialism.

Haeckel hated Christianity, and rightly saw evolution as incompatible with Christian doctrine. His teaching has come into disrepute, for in his later years he was found guilty in a university trial of fraudulently tampering with his data — data he used with great effectiveness to validate and teach evolution.

Haeckel was the main advocate of the concept of embryonic recapitulation, that the human embryo recapitulates (or remembers) its evolutionary past.

Superficial resemblances can be seen between the embryos of various organisms. Obviously, even the human embryo starts out as a single cell, resembling a single-celled organism. According to Haeckel, as it develops, a sac is attached to the embryo which is like the yolk sac of a bird. At one point, the embryo has linear folds that he indicated look like "gill slits" in a fish embryo. Soon the embryo develops a tail-like structure, which was a leftover from the animals. He even fudged his drawings to make the embryos look more alike, and it was for this he was tried and convicted.

We now know that in all cases of comparison and similarity he was wrong.[11] The "yolk sac" supplies blood cells to the

---

11 Wilburt H. Rusch, "Ontgeny Recapitulates Phylogeny," *Creation Research Society Quarterly*, June 1969, p. 27–34.

growing embryo, a very necessary function. The "gill slits" in the human turn out to be neither gills nor slits. Gills are used for breathing, but never do these folds open into the throat or lungs. Rather, they develop into essential parts of the human ear, and the parathyroid and thymus glands. The folds are the not-yet-finished displays of vital human parts. The "tail" develops into the human coccyx, or "tail bone." Far from being a useless or leftover vestige, the coccyx anchors the muscles of the hips and legs, attaching them to the spinal column, without which human posture and movements would be impossible.

In recent years, medical science has developed ways to monitor the growing embryo, and has concluded that every aspect of the human fetus, at every stage of its development, is distinctly and uniquely human. Today, Haeckel's theory has been totally discredited, however strongly it remains in the folklore of evolution.

We now turn our attention to the only other category of scientific evidence presented for human evolution, that of the fossils. A look at each one of the supposed ape-human transitions reveals absolutely no evidence for human evolution.

Neanderthal Man

Early Darwinists desperately sought fossil evidence that man had come from the apes. Darwin had reported that none was available at the time he published *The Origin of the Species* in 1859. Over the next four decades, however, a number of remains were found which were used in the Scopes trial.

Neanderthal skull

The first scrap of skull was found in a German cave near the Neander Valley in 1857, but was not generally known until other more complete skeletons of Neanderthal surfaced. Medical experts of the day were convinced that Neanderthal Man, as he came to be known in the popular press, was totally human, although suffering from pathological problems, most notably rickets and arthritis. The skull sported a heavy brow ridge, and a thigh bone was curved; otherwise Neanderthal was fully human.

As other specimens were collected, typical Neanderthal features also included a low forehead, heavy lower jaw, a meager chin, and rather heavily built bones. Bones with those characteristics were also found in Asia and Africa, as well as Europe.

A nearly complete skeleton found in 1908 allowed Professor Marcellin Boule to reconstruct the entire anatomy, and he went on to propose a lifestyle based on his evolutionary presuppositions. He concocted a brutish ape-man, bow-legged and stoop-shouldered, and always totally naked. His reconstruction served to brainwash many into believing in evolution, including the "experts" testifying or reporting on the Scopes trial.

As is so often the case, the facts came out too late, after the damage had been done. Neanderthals, it is now known, had a cranial capacity which exceeded the average human today. They buried their dead with religious significance, and were probably the source of at least some cave drawings. They crafted and used tools, cultivated crops, and no doubt had a spoken language. Some evidence exists of record-keeping, musical instruments, weapons, and possible writing. These were totally human individuals.

In adult specimens, the teeth were crowded forward, in addition to the other physical characteristics. But it has been noted that all of these features are not dissimilar to those of very old individuals living today. The children's fossils give evidence of having matured late as well.

Creationists have long suspected that the Neanderthals were an ethnic group who migrated away from the incident at the Tower of Babel, complete with a language, but perhaps little technology. Soon they found themselves in harsh, European, ice-age conditions, and were forced to eke out a living with poor nutrition, living in caves. But according to Scripture, in the early generations following the flood, people still lived to great ages. Perhaps Neanderthal typical features were due to a very long life, up to several hundred years long.

Furthermore, we now know that Neanderthal-like features are still with us. Some experts think that Neanderthals are today's east Europeans. A tribe of Filipinos show similar characteristics. Once a full skeleton of a knight buried in a full suit of armor was found to have the typical Neanderthal body style.

While there may have been some justification for citing the Neanderthals at the Scopes trial, there is no longer such justification. Neanderthal Man was fully human, a fact recognized today by all scientists, even evolutionists.[12] Unfortunately, Nean-

---

12 Boyce Rensberger, "Facing the Past," *Science 81*, October 1981.

derthal still appears in textbooks and museums as an ape-man, especially in the minds of the public.

Homo Erectus

Homo erectus has come to be a catch-all category for quite a number of human-like fossils that have something about them to suggest a connection with the apes. At the time of the Scopes trial, the only one available was a specimen from Java, found by Eugene Dubois in 1891.

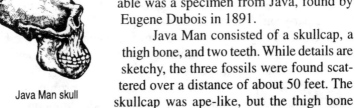

Java Man skull

Java Man consisted of a skullcap, a thigh bone, and two teeth. While details are sketchy, the three fossils were found scattered over a distance of about 50 feet. The skullcap was ape-like, but the thigh bone pointed to an erect posture, and was indistinguishable from a human femur. Dubois convinced himself that the several bones were from the same individual creature. He originally called it a man-like ape, but, recognizing the femur as totally human-like, in 1893 he changed it to an ape-like man.

His discovery was greeted with much skepticism in scientific circles, with many questioning if his fossils were from the same individual. His ensuing career was spent defending his position. However, there were a few surprises along the way.

In 1889, before he found his Java Man, he had discovered two skulls, fully human, in rocks dated older than those in which he found Java Man. Here was his problem: If modern man was older than Java Man, then Java Man was not the ancestor of modern man. So he hid the two human skulls under the floorboards of his home for 30 years, finally reporting them to increase his sagging popularity.

More discoveries were eventually found in Java, and in 1935 Dubois published his conclusion that the original skullcap was identical to that of a gibbon-like ape. An ape skull and a human femur — not very good evidence to present at the trial.

The evidence is even worse now, for numerous *Homo erectus* specimens have been found — complete with tools and indications of the use of fire — all evidence that they were truly human.[13] Despite the checkered past and the recent reassignment

---

13 Marvin L. Lubenow, *Bones of Contention* (Grand Rapids, MI: Baker Book House, 1992).

to the genus *Homo*, many leading evolutionists and public school textbooks still use Java Man as prime evidence that man evolved from the apes.

Piltdown Man

From 1908 to 1912 the "true" ape-man was found, and this was to be a cornerstone of the ACLU Scopes case. This fossil consisted of parts of a human skull and most of the jaw of an ape. Here was proof that the apes had evolved a large brain, and were clearly on their way to becoming human. The fragments were discovered just a few miles from Darwin's old home by Professor Arthur Keith, an aggressively committed evolutionist.

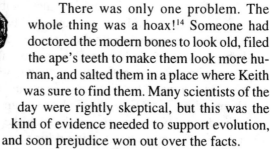

There was only one problem. The whole thing was a hoax![14] Someone had doctored the modern bones to look old, filed the ape's teeth to make them look more human, and salted them in a place where Keith was sure to find them. Many scientists of the day were rightly skeptical, but this was the kind of evidence needed to support evolution, and soon prejudice won out over the facts.

Piltdown fossils

The fraud was finally admitted in 1953, long after the Scopes trial, and long after textbooks had indoctrinated two generations of students. A world of experts had studied these fossils, over 50 Ph.D. dissertations had been published, and no one reported the unlikely staining, or the file marks evident on the teeth. Several theories exist as to who perpetrated the fraud, including some of the biggest evolutionary scientists of the day, but the mystery remains. But there is no mystery as to how such obviously fraudulently doctored bones could fool the world's greatest experts for 40 years. They must have wanted desperately to see ape-like characteristics in the human skull, and human-like characteristics in the ape jaw, and they succeeded.

Nebraska Man

In 1922 America proclaimed its own fossil man, when a single molar was found in Nebraska. Though it was only a single tooth, Professor Henry Fairfield Osborn, head of the prestigious

---

14 S.J. Gould, *Natural History,* vol. 88 (1979), p. 96.

American Museum of Natural History in New York City, declared it to be man's early ancestor. Officially called *Hesperopithecus*, Nebraska Man was an immediate hit, complete with a two-page spread in the *Illustrated London News*.[15]

From a single tooth was drawn a whole family. The naked ape-man, sporting his club, was flanked by his naked wife gathering roots for supper. Behind them were a herd of camels and a herd of horses, whose fossils had been found in the same deposit, but were extinct in that location long ago. The imaginative newspaper coverage and the timing of the find made a big impression at the 1925 Scopes trial. Nebraska Man was never introduced into the trial, since the lead paleoanthropologist, Dr. Fay Cooper Cole, had some misgivings about it, but it was there nonetheless.

Shortly after the trial, some more fossil bones of the owner of the tooth were found, and it was not human after all.[16] Rather, an extinct variety of pig had been on display. To make matters worse, in 1972 the pig variety was found still alive in Paraguay. As ICR's Dr. Duane Gish likes to say, "This is a case where an evolutionist made a man out of a pig, and a pig made a monkey out of a man."

Australopithecus

This name will be recognized by all students of today, for current opinion is that modern man evolved in Africa, and many recent finds are considered in this genus. The original find and

the name go back to Dr. Raymond Dart, who in 1924 found the face and lower jaw of a young ape in South Africa. He dubbed the find a missing link, *Australopithecus africanus,* ape-man of South Africa. It has come to be known as the Taung Child, after the quarry in which it was found.

Australopithecus Africanus fossil.

The discovery itself generated little but controversy, but it was found within months of the Scopes trial, and received much attention by the American press. The expert testimony expressed uncertainty and caution, but such was not in the newspaper reports.

---

15 *Illustrated London News,* June 24, 1922.
16 W.K. Gregory, *Science,* vol. 66 (1927), p. 579.

Scientists know that attaching too much significance to details in a juvenile's skull can be risky. Newborn apes have an eerie human appearance to them. Further development erases the similarity.

Dart's Taung Child is dismissed these days by many as that of a young ape, but the hunt for African fossils was on, and continues today, with Drs. Louis and Mary Leakey, their son Richard Leakey, and Drs. Donald Johannson and Tim White playing central roles. Undoubtedly, the most notoriety was given to Johannson's 1974 discovery of "Lucy," *Australopithecus afarensis.* While most fossil discoveries are extremely fragmentary, "Lucy" was 40 percent complete, and warrants description.

Considered a female, she stood less than 3-1/2 feet tall. Her skull was not found, but a portion of the lower jaw was fully ape-like. Other *Australopithecus* fossils have all been fully ape from the neck up, with cranial capacity in the range of chimps. From the neck down, "Lucy" had two features which suggested that she walked more erect than other apes, and thus was a "missing link."

If the hip is viewed from a certain angle, it appeared (to Johannson at least) that it allowed a slightly more erect posture. Other investigators,[17] studying these and other remains with more sophisticated methods, disagree. Furthermore, "Lucy's" knee joint hints at more erect posture, but, again, other experts disagree, and much question has been raised as to the discovery location of the proposed knee joint. Was it in the same area? Many think not, but the truth is hard to ferret out.

But even if the knee belongs with the rest of Lucy, and both knee and hip allow more erect posture, we still have a chimp-sized ape, with long, curved fingers and toes, just right for swinging in trees. It appears that these creatures were apes, perhaps an extinct species of ape, but not in the line of humans.

The charade continues, with funding, fame, and enormous egos at stake. A recent announcement by White told of his discovery of 17 fragments of bone, none bigger than a man's fingernail. A chip from the elbow impressed him that this creature walked a little less erect than "Lucy"; therefore, it was a still earlier ancestor of man.

Other discoveries could be discussed, dating since the

---

17 J.T. Stern and R.L. Susman, "The Locomotor Anatomy of *A. Afarensis,*" *American Journal of Physical Anthropology,* vol. 60, p. 279–318.

Scopes trial, but suffice it here to note that of the five evidences in question in 1925, one was a hoax, one an ape, two (at least) perfectly human, and one a pig. The biggest victory for evolution was built on false leads, and things have improved little since.

For Further Reading

For more detailed discussion of the scientific evidences for creation, as well as documentation from the standard scientific literature, the reader may wish to consult one or more of the following books, all available from the Institute for Creation Research, P.O. Box 2667; El Cajon, California, 92021.

The Young Earth by John D. Morris (202 pages), $12.95.

Scientific Creationism by Henry M. Morris (281 pages), $8.95.

Evolution: Challenge of the Fossil Record by Duane T. Gish (277 pages), $8.95.

What is Creation Science? by Henry M. Morris and Gary E. Parker (336 pages), $10.95.

The Origin of Species Revisited by Wendell R. Bird (2 volumes, 1,149 pages), $59.95.

Bones of Contention by Marvin Lubenow (295 pages), $12.95.

Creation Scientists Answer Their Critics by Duane T. Gish (451 pages), $16.95.

CHAPTER 4

THE EFFECT OF THE EVOLUTION "VICTORY"

by John D. Morris

The stakes are high in the creation/evolution controversy. If creation is true, and mankind is created in the image of God, then He has the authority to set the rules over our lives and lifestyles, and the authority to set the penalty for breaking the rules. There is such a thing as absolute truth, right and wrong. Our responsibility is to submit to His kingship over our lives, and obey His teachings.

But what if we evolved from the apes, merely by chance mutations? No one sets the rules over our lives; there are no absolutes, no standards to live by. We can live as we choose. In evolution, only survival and reproduction are important; added to this is the lure of satisfying one's "animal" desires. "Few animals mate for life; we are animals, so why should we limit our sexual freedom? There is no meaning to life, just do what you want."

Jesus told Nicodemus, "If I have told you earthly things [i.e., about creation], and ye believe not, how shall ye believe, if I tell you of heavenly things" (John 3:12). Earthly things can be observed and verified, such as the strong evidence for creation as opposed to the almost non-existent evidence for evolution. But if we choose not to believe the well-verified evidence from creation and history, can we expect God to be truthful when He tells us that we can have forgiveness of sins based on His death on the cross? "The wages of sin is death" (Rom. 6:33), but "Christ died for our sins" (1 Cor. 15:3). On what basis can we trust Him when He offers us eternal life with Him in heaven if we receive His free gift of salvation? Because we see His Word so verified as we look at "earthly things," our confidence grows in His teaching of "heavenly things" that are beyond our ability to verify.

"Why do so many reject this truth, if the evidence is so convincing?" one might ask. Jesus continues: "This is the condemnation, that light is come into the world, and men loved darkness rather than light, because their deeds were evil" (John 3:19). You see, one's chosen lifestyle is the issue. Many have rejected God's free offer of forgiveness, salvation, and eternal life because they know they would need to change their habits. But be not deceived, one cannot forever enjoy the "pleasures of sin" (Heb. 11:25). "There is a way which seemeth right unto a man, but the end thereof are the ways of death" (Prov. 14:12). How much better to embrace the light, rather than cling to the darkness of wrong choices.

In the same conversation with Nicodemus, an honest seeker of truth, Jesus explained how one can move from darkness to light. "For God so loved the world, that He gave His only begotten Son, that whosoever believeth in Him should not perish, but have everlasting life" (John 3:16). God the Father willingly sent God the Son to earth on our behalf. The penalty for our sin was death, eternal separation from God. But God so loved us that His Son was sent to die as a sacrifice, paying the penalty for our sin. "Even so must the Son of man be lifted up" (John 3:14) on the cross of Calvary, "that whosoever believeth in Him should not perish, but have eternal life" (John 3:15).

To "believe" in Him is to have faith in Him: faith that His death satisfied God's holy justice and substituted for our death. This is one of those "heavenly things" that we cannot experimentally verify as we can the "earthly things," but we have faith that our faith is a reasonable faith.

Becoming a Christian involves this transaction: simply receiving God's free gift of forgiveness and salvation, based on the fact that the penalty has already been paid — Christ's death applied to our penalty. In His grace, He extends to us "everlasting life," a life in heaven with Him that will never end.

Dear friend, please don't reject this free gift, don't choose darkness rather than light. Don't accept the condemnation of God simply to preserve a sinful lifestyle. "He that believeth on Him is not condemned; but he that believeth not is condemned already, because he hath not believed in the name of the only begotten Son of God" (John 3:18).